Books by Howard Moss

POEMS
Buried City   1975
Selected Poems   1971
Second Nature   1968
Finding Them Lost   1965
A Winter Come, A Summer Gone   1960
A Swimmer in the Air   1957
The Toy Fair   1954
The Wound and the Weather   1946

LIGHT VERSE
A Swim off the Rocks   1976

CRITICISM
Writing Against Time   1969
The Magic Lantern of Marcel Proust   1962

EDITED, WITH AN INTRODUCTION
The Poet's Story   1973
The Nonsense Books of Edward Lear   1964
Keats   1959

SATIRE
Instant Lives   1974

A Swim off the Rocks

A Swim off the Rocks

Light Verse by Howard Moss

New York Atheneum *1976*

The following poems first appeared in *The New Yorker: A Swim Off the Rocks, Tourists, Geography: A Song, Bermuda, Elizabethan Tragedy: A Footnote, Tennis: A Portrait, Small Elegy, The Skaters' Waltz, The End of Words: An Election-Year Thought, Charm, The Refrigerator, Companies, Circle, A Thank-You Note for Imaginary Gifts*.

Other poems first appeared in *Boston University Journal*, CAIM, *Commentary, The Georgia Review, Hampden-Sydney Poetry Review, Harper's, Harper's Bazaar, Hika, Marilyn, The Nation, New American Writing, The New Republic, New Letters, Pebble, Shenandoah, The Transatlantic Review*.

Library of Congress Cataloging in Publication Data
Moss, Howard, 1922-
    A swim off the rocks.
    Poems.
    I. Title.
PS3525.O8638S75   811./5/4   76-15055
ISBN 0-689-10763-3 pbk.

For Joseph Caldwell *and* Van Varner

Contents

IV

V

I

A Swim off the Rocks

A flat rock is the best for taking off.
  Rafferty, the lawyer, with a cough,
    Goes first, head first—a dive
That makes us wonder how he's still alive!
  The ballerina's next, and shames us all.
What grace in space! What an Australian crawl!

I'm next—and too self-conscious to be good.
  When I look back to where I stood,
    Miss Jones, a leather crafter,
Has run, jumped in, and made it to the raft. Her
Body salty-white, she stares back at the shore, a
Lot like Lot's wife in Sodom and Gomorrah.

The ballerina knows how much restraint
  Enhances skill and, with a little feint,
    Spins away. Now Rafferty
Appears to be arguing a case at sea.
Splashing, gesticulating, he swims back,
And climbs, exhausted, onto the rock.

Miss Jones comes in—martyred, ill at ease,
  And towels carefully, even knees,
    While the lawyer fetches beer.
The dancer always seems to disappear.
Miss Jones, sotto-voce: "It's *said*, in *town*,
She's found a choreographer all her own."

What *I* say, though, is let what *is* just be.
  Miss Jones and Mr. Rafferty—
    A hopeless combination—
Have my good wishes for a grand vacation.
The dancer needs no help, evidently.
And as for me, I simply like the sea.

Geography: A Song

There are no rocks
At Rockaway,
There are no sheep
At Sheepshead Bay,
There's nothing new
In Newfoundland,
And silent is
Long Island Sound.

Bermuda

Beach house, cabana, bungalow, hotel,
Your walls are weathered by a warped pastel
   Too delicate for seagulls to detect;
   The run-on blues, the pinkish wrecks
Rattle the air in plaster, coral,
While listless birds attack a wall,
   Adding themselves to the dim graffiti,
   Sometimes obscene, and sometimes witty.

Each morning the landscape seems to be drugged.
Could that quiet bay, overnight, have dragged
   The sea's museum for its salty tortures?
   What we see from widow's walks and porches
Is a coastal life of minute reversals;
An orange mothering a withered eel,
   Dead coral hardened to the finest brain,
   And primary colors, after the rain.

The tourist searches for his private symbol,
Vaguely hostile, like a water pistol.
   Which is suspicious? Which is correct?
   A mirror fragment on the whirling back
Of a Negro dancer, or the plush décor
Of an Empire widow serving tea at four?
   Scrawled in chalk in an alleyway:
   "Shoeshine 10c As Good As Broadway."

Contradiction in terms: a stageset struck
By lightning, the trees a deaf-mute's joke
   Told too fast. Then its point gets lost
   Completely. Thunder. And the rain at last . . .
The sea's catastrophes are witticisms
Heard from a distance, over littered miles.
   How can we believe in its total horror,
   This hurricane in an ice-cream parlor?

From steeples made of papier-maché
The bell tongues clang, "Relent, Relent"—
     As if the sea could condemn or pardon
     Itself, the weather, or this crazy garden.
At five o'clock, what the wind is doing
Is semitropical brewing, brewing,
     Now calm, now furied, as if, as it went,
     It would push its finger through a monument.

A Western Piano: Middle Age

The frontier accordion has settled down
Into domestic bliss and grown
Fat on its woodwork and gold lettering.

In spite of the passion that can wring it dry,
It is full of terrible puns—a kind
Of peasant gaiety embarrassing

To the wit inherent in its *schwarmerei*.
Broadening and cracked, it has a soul.
In fact, it is the very soul of soul.

It likes to sing *"O bel mio* . . .
I am mellow, mellow, mellow, mellow . . ."
Whose songs get younger as the years go by.

Rye, In Winter

There are amusement parks so elegant
They no longer amuse. In Rye, the scene
In winter—with its stucco Moorish cant,
Its unused rides—is out of Graham Greene.

Pleasure's sinister. Sometimes the best
Architecture brings to mind a kill
Under the boardwalk. A corpse, undressed,
Is fashion going to the dogs. A gull,

Single, clerical, circles at first
The administration building, then the Sound,
But, a true scavenger, alights at last
On the Rest Rooms open the year round.

Tourists

Cramped like sardines on the Queens, and sedated,
The sittings all first, the roommates mismated,

Three nuns at the table, the waiter a barber,
Then dumped with their luggage at some frumpish harbor,

Veering through rapids in a vapid *rapido*
To view the new moon from a ruin on the Lido,

Or a sundown in London from a rundown Mercedes,
Then high-borne to Glyndebourne for Orfeo in Hades,

Embarrassed in Paris in Harris tweed, dying to
Get to the next museum piece that they're flying to,

Finding, in Frankfurt, that one indigestible
Comestible makes them too ill for the Festival,

Footloose in Lucerne, or taking a pub in in
Stratford or Glasgow, or maudlin in Dublin, in-

sensitive, garrulous, querulous, audible,
Drunk in the Dolomites, tuning a portable,

Homesick in Stockholm, or dressed to toboggan
At the wrong time of year in too dear Copenhagen,

Generally being too genial or hostile—
Too grand at the Grand, too old at the Hostel—

Humdrum conundrums, what's to become of them?
Most will come home, but there will be some of them

Subsiding like Lawrence in Florence, or crazily
Ending up tending shop up in Fiesole.

Venezia: A Footnote

Tómbola on the piazza,
Gondolas on the Canal,
Ravioli in the trattória,
Disentario at the Hotel.

A Rented Sail

Here on this little plank
With its handkerchief of sail,
I hear the minor spank
Of water and the wail
Of faroff engines. Thank
God I'm here. Words fail . . .

Winds, too. Not outward bound
But merely maritime,
How happily I sound
The depths of the sublime
By sitting on the Sound,
A waterwing of time!

There is a blue rock,
There a rubescent tree.
I hardly move. I rock
The drifts monotonously.
Now, still as a shipwreck,
The sun is on to me.

To wash salt sweat away
With salt, I dip my copper
Dipper down halfway
And splash myself. A proper
Wind's up. On the way
Home, I eat my supper.

This leaky, rented boat
From which I caught no scup—
One blowfish with the bloat
Was all I totted up—
I tote back to its float.
At six, the jig is up.

II

Elizabethan Tragedy: A Footnote

That prudent Prince who ends Shakespearian plays
And wanders in to tell us how we wasted time
To hate or fall in love or be deranged
Would, three hours earlier, have ruined the play.
And so experience is, after all,
The heart of the matter. Even chatter
And babbling, or scenes in the worst of love affairs,
Like tears or throwing things or being pushed downstairs,
Have value in the long run. Caution has its place.
Premeditation, though, I think when face to face
With *sturm und drang* can never win the race.
Although the Prince is on the angels' side,
What got him there is wholesale homicide.

A Song Struck from the Records

Dear fairy Godmother, hold back
   Your magic transformation;
I see a coming cul-de-sac
   In rising above my station:
I know my clothes are awful, my
   Room a mess, but then,
At least I'm not surrounded by
   Secret Service men.
I fear the Prince's hunting lodge,
   I fear, my dear, his mother;
Frankly, I hate the whole hodgepodge,
   And the infernal bother.

No Prince falls short of the ideal
   Except on close inspection,
And royal houses, once they're real,
   Reveal some imperfection:
The widest moat, so crystal clear
   Today, becomes tomorrow
A muddy ditch with scummed veneer,
   Incredibly more narrow.
I'd be, should you invoke your wand,
   More sinned against than sinning,
And sadder at the happy end
   Than at the sad beginning.

The Writer at the End of the Bar

Dated at forty-five? Not yet,
You sly, old Phoenix in leather boots.
Infancy with its double takes
Is your seismograph and its earthquakes.
Tell me, what are you writing now—
My Damaged Nerves: The Great Shakes?

Dumbshows count, not words. You are
Silent, maimed. Slumped at a bar,
What's left to learn in its mirrored length
That isn't already mirrored at length
In your life? Is it true you are
Writing, *Oh, God Give Me Strength—*

The Weak Shall Inherit Each Other?
They'd better; they don't inherit the earth.
Sometimes they don't—or can't, or won't—
Even inherit each other. So
Why revise *The Prodigal Sons:*
No Deposits And No Returns?

Get up, get out. Night's dark and cheap.
Hell is a place that's never filled.
Maybe that's where you'll sleep tonight,
Writing in dreams, as the sleeve unravels
Your latest non-best-seller,
Down In The Dumps and Other Travels.

Hansel and Gretel

To be baked as cookies by the mad witch?
Not so funny. See *The Rise and Fall*
Of the Third Reich. What starts out as kitsch
All too soon becomes a form of evil.

The witch was wise. What sweet tooth can resist
A candy cottage? They were wiser still,
Scattering their breadcrumbs not to get lost.
How could the witch know that they were trained to kill?

They got back home all right, the cunning children,
Only to end up in Munich, years later,
Stirring up the witchcraft of their own cauldron,
She a drunk and he a sadistic waiter.

"Maybe it would have been better," she said,
One day in her cups, "to have roasted in the oven
Than to hobble around this city, half dead—
Old movie stars in some dreary love-in."

At which he struck her. "Peasant . . . *peasant!*"
Then, lunging toward her, "You ungrateful bitch!
I wasted my life on our stupid legend
When my one and only love was the dead witch."

Proust at the Ritz

"Sometimes he went out at 2 A.M. to see if anyone was still attending a dinner party he had ordered to be given at the Ritz."

Nostalgia, A Psychoanalytical
Study of Marcel Proust by MILTON L. MILLER

Some say
The *pommes soufflés*
Produced by Proust
At the Ritz one day,
Along with the broiled *langoustes,*
Were devoured (to many *mots justes*)
By the *crême de la société.*

"It is all much too *de trop*—
Even my *quiche*
Seems *nouveau riche,*"
Said a guest when Proust didn't show.
"Our nervous, asthmatic host
Is a genius, and here's a toast.
But the person he cares for most

(The affair will never last)
Doesn't give one *sou*
And won't get through
A la Recherche du Temps Perdu—
Or how you say
In good *anglais,*
The *Remembrance of Things Past*?"

Modified Sonnets

(Dedicated to adapters, abridgers, digesters, and condensers everywhere)

SHALL I COMPARE THEE TO A SUMMER'S DAY?

Who says you're like one of the dog days?
You're nicer. And better.
Even in May, the weather can be gray,
And a summer sub-let doesn't last forever.
Sometimes the sun's too hot;
Sometimes it is not.
Who can stay young forever?
People break their necks or just drop dead!
But you? Never!
If there's just one condensed reader left
Who can figure out the abridged alphabet,
After you're dead and gone,
In this poem you'll live on!

MUSIC TO HEAR, WHY HEAR'ST THOU MUSIC SADLY?

Why are you listening to the radio, crying?
The program's good. You're nice. What could be wrong?
If you don't like it, why don't you try dialling?
Why keep humming if you don't like the song?
You're tuned in to the best jazz, rock, and classical
The unions make. If you don't like 'em,
Try, they're not bad, just a bit nonsensical.
Or maybe it's that you'd like to be alone? H'mmn?
Listen, it's as good as Kostelanetz!
You know what tone he gets out of the strings.
They sound like a happy family. Honest.
Like when the kids sing what the mother sings.
There's a lesson in it, though. Hear that tone?
One person couldn't do it. Don't live alone!

When I'm out of cash and full of shame,
And crying to beat the band, alone,
And even God doesn't know my name,
And all I do is weep and moan,
I curse myself in the mirror,
Wishing I had a future,
Or some real pals, or was a good looker,
Or even a crazy artist or a deep thinker!
As I said, when even the old kicks seem tame,
And just when I hate myself the most,
I think about you. Then I'm o.k.
Just like a bird who hates the dirt
And can fly in the sky to get away.
    Thinking of you is as good as money.
    I'd give up royalties for you, honey.

The Sunlight Sonata

*"What I did for Beethoven I can do for you! One after-
noon, as I sat all alone listening to Beethoven's Ninth, I
got to thinking what sheer genius the man must have had
to accomplish so much under such primitive working
conditions—handicapped by clutter, poor workspace,
drafts, noise and bad lighting. So . . . I picked up my
sketch pad—just for fun—and designed the poor fellow
an office worthy of his greatness, with every detail as
personal as his scrawl on a manuscript. Ludwig, I
think, would have been happy here . . ."*

Advertisement in *The New Yorker* for an
office designed by GEORGE W. REINOEHL

"Ludwig, are you decent, dear?   *Beethoven's housekeeper*
Mr. George Reinoehl is here.   *shouts up the stairwell.*
His designs look awfully queer.
Come down, Ludwig, do you hear!

"Ludwig's not too well, I fear.   *She entertains*
He's been drinking tons of beer.   *Mr. Reinoehl.*
Please don't mention Meyerbeer.
Ludwig, are you coming, dear?

"See these pretty plans? They're   *She tries to convince*
   sheer   *Beethoven of the*
Heaven! When he wrote *King*   *feasibility and beauty of*
   Lear,   *Mr. Reinoehl's plans.*
What helped Shakespeare persevere
Was an office full of cheer.

"Dante, the Italian seer,
Used to love to dree his weir-
ds in a workroom as severe—
The décor kept his thinking clear.

"Ludwig says it's too austere.
The painting doesn't seem sincere.
The walnut has the wrong veneer.
The tone is thin on the clavier.

*She confers with
Beethoven and reports
his reactions.*

"A radio! O pioneer!
It's so clever to appear
Something like two hundred year-
s before it was invented. Dear

*She is overcome by a
gadget.*

"Ludwig, put away that spear!
(I think you'd better disappear!)"
"No drafts? No noise? *Mein Gott!
Weh's mir!*
I would NOT be happy here!"

*Beethoven becomes
incensed. She warns
Mr. Reinoehl away.
Beethoven speaks.*

*Beethoven tears up the
blueprints and writes
the Sixth, Seventh,
Eighth, and Ninth
Symphonies.*

Three Double Dactyls

1

Tra-la-la tra-la-la,
Sergei Rachmaninoff,
Humming some tunes that he
Heard in his head,

Suddenly stiffened and,
Uncontrapuntally,
Wrote them all down as the
"Isle of the Dead."

2

Pocketa-pocketa,
Sergei Diaghilev,
Seeing the tennis net
Set up for "Jeux,"

Said to Debussy,—
"Impressionistically—
Isn't that tennis court
Tilted, *un peu*?"

3

Higgledy-piggledy,
Emily Dickinson,
Fed up with Amherst, de-
cided to roam

East to the Baltics. "This
Czechoslovakian
Goulash is awful," she
Said. "Let's go home."

Herons

(For the 77th birthday of Marianne Moore)

Our largest common wader,
      the Great
  Blue Heron's distinct because of its size;
With a slow and regular wing beat, it flies
  With its feet extended beyond it in flight.
Bare-skinned between its bill and eyes—
  Its thin beak yellow, sharp, and straight—
It usually nests in colonies,
  But when the heron starts to soar,
It cries, "More, more! More Marianne Moore!"
  Quoth the heron, "Marianne Moore."

The common eastern heron,
      the Green
  Heron is scarcely bigger than a crow.
Its typical heron wing-stroke's slow,
  Its legs are distinctly orange-yellow.
It raises its crest in pique or alarm,
  Its middle toenail, edged with a comb,
Looks like a pen with a quill and a plume,
  And when the heron comes ashore,
It cries, "More, more! More Marianne Moore!"
  Quoth the heron, "Marianne Moore."

III

Tennis: A Portrait

Always careful not to be kind
In case the network of demand
Bind you fast and, falsely bound,
Pity or rage shoot your backhand

Into the net, you will not play
This game or any other. Let
Fools who win have their dog's day;
Your triumph is to watch the set

From the sidelines while you cheer the serves
Smashed over by the stupid young.
They do not know how the wind swerves
The best-aimed shot from its target. Stung

By age, high-strung among the doubles, only
You are single. They miss the mark,
Your verbal strokes—each lob, each volley
As bright, and seedy, as New York, New York.

You know the score—your nets of wit
Hide your fine hand and, hand in glove,
Time's racket lays no bets on it,
Though it was once, at thirty, love.

A Small Vision at a Large Party

Now that everyone's
Head is drumming
With gin and vermouth,
Look there, coming

Down the stairs,
Putting on airs,
Is Midas among
The millionaires.

Fern Dying

I left it in the mailbox an entire day,
The latest note from Madame Blank who writes,
"Expect nothing, dear. You won't be disappointed."
I read it wolfing down my frozen dinner
Tasting so full of chemicals it might
Well be a form of dry shampoo reshaped,
How cleverly! into this turkey loaf
I scrape away—to join its chef, I hope.

I walk outside onto the moonless terrace.
Conservatory sounds: FM, TV,
The new urban music—gunshots, sirens,
Air-conditioners, exhausted, vented . . .
How sad the lighted trees in these environs!
If they could make a wish, they'd be transplanted

—And so would I.

A Francophile whose style
Is the ultimate Morse Code in dots and dashes,
Madame underlines her words for emphasis:

"Here are my versions of some René Char
Poems . . . Be *frank*! *Tell* me—are they *good*?
Or *bad*, as the case may be! Don't spare
The rod! And here's my essay on Cocteau
(We were too *close* for him to mention me . . .)—
It's *still* unpublished! Tell me . . . *really*! *Why?*"

And so on. So forth. Blah, blah. Then,
Ending with a postscript *interruptus*:

"Goodbye, my dear, until we meet again . . .
I trust I can count on an *early* opinion? . . .
I'll call on Wednesday to arrange just *when* . . ."

On my desk my Boston fern is dying
From rot or heat, brown-leaved, tobacco-tongued,
Too dry, too wet, impossible to know . . .
Sometimes I wish that plants would find their voice
As I've found mine, coaxing one to grow;
I've sung to it, addressed it with commands
Brown thumbs resort to trying to be green—
Bloom! Bloom! Like Molly in *Ulysses*. Joyce.
A spore is not a flower. Jean Cocteau?

I sound like Madame Blank. I mean between
The lines . . . Or in them. That old pathetic bore!
That dying generation with no song!
And with that, unexpected tears. Poor lady!
Poor fern! The room is gravid with self-pity.
My ballpoint pen is writing something:
                                    "Dear
Madame Blank,
            Wednesday will be fine . . ."

A Colloquy with Gregory
on the Balcony

Now tell me again about Miss Teller's dog.
You were up on the balcony? Yes? And then?
You felt an irresistible desire to smash . . .
Oh, *push*. I'm sorry. I see. And when
The moon shone down on her leg like satin
So even the finest porous nylon
Thickened with longing . . . Something snapped?
A synapse, perhaps? The mind has traps . . .
I'm *not* attacking you. I see what you mean:
The moon changes things. I've been affected myself.
I *am* affected? I didn't come here to be . . .
If you feel that way, why I think I'll be . . .
No, no, forget that. This is all so ghastly!
Of *course*, I support you. Now take it ea . . .
Naturally I respect your desire to be
*Some*body. I'm with you all the way,
In spite of the sordid . . . Yes. I mean
If you try real hard you can often see
Why people are crazy . . . Gregory, plea-
se, get back inside! I was pulling your leg!
Be reasonable! Stop! For God's sake! *Greg!* . . .

Three Dances from the *Daily News*

Yes it was you, Juarez,
Who, arriving in a daze
To take Dolores out
In your red Volks runabout
(Your outfit was a gem:
Half Barney's, half Jerusalem),
Said, in a kind of shout,
"Jeezus, let's get the hell out!"
Oh, touring was a delight
With Dolores, that sybarite,
To whom the greatest pleasure was
Thumbing her nose at the fuzz.
(Her dream: religious, porous—
A holy, bullet-holed Dolores.)
Thanks (a lot!) to her, they got
You in the end in a vacant lot,
Those finks, Ed and Jimmy,
Each an oldtime enemy,
And though they laid Dolores twice,
Took your bread and took her ice,
They shot you but not her,
For she was a conspirator
To lure you out of the city
Whenever they were ready.
So, Juarez, goodbye, you poor
Bastard only your mother mourns for.

WALTZ: DOWN AT THE DOCKS

From listening
To the strains
Of waltzes
In the grand salons,

The rats
Have got
Vienna
In their veins.

PAVANE: THE EAST SIDE

When Countess Mara and Bronzini meet
At Madison and Fifty-seventh Street,
The fashion ads turn into Klees
And Orbach's into Mainbocher's.

Rusty

Hot *what* in the hot rod just sped by
The lights, direct grass? Violences?
Caught in the stucco: words and lines
Scrawled on the toilet walls, or scrawled
In Spanish on a white wall (but that was
In another country.) That was Mind,
Rusty's mind, made up of trips
To sex and back, but in the comic strips.
"I never minded what they said," he said,
"I never minded it at all," he said,
And raced through shantytown and out of it.
Was he the self-destructive principle?
What killed him? Rusty! What killed *you*?
Those languid mornings at the A. and P.,
The lettuce leaves breathing the country,
The dirt that clung to every carrot root,
The sawdust like a circus underfoot,
And all for money, money, money . . .?
"Oh, not for money," Rusty would say,
"Oh, no, no, no! I did it all for love."

Small Elegy

In the smart room where Lennie lies,
French draperies are too silk for eyes
That like their hangings plain, like their ties
Thin-striped. Lennie will no more arise

And go now where the cocktail shakers shake
Their crystal energies and pianists fake
Some lovelorn valentines and, on the make,
Mirrored faces join, and part, and break.

And since those wretched limbs, not custom-made
But real and common, in a last charade
Crumble into peace, who's to parade
Up Fifth and down with all his tricks of trade?

The chandelier, the chiffonier, the waste
By-products of the golden calf, Good Taste,
Surround his body. To his Never-Faced-
Reality, gentlemen, a final toast!

Damn it, he had good taste! That's all he had.
He knew the nearly-good from the not-quite-bad.
Lennie wore the first vest made of plaid.
Lennie gave it up when it became a fad.

Goodbye, Lennie—fad, plaid, and Madras!
May artificial angels and high brass
Proclaim a high-fidelity Mass
When you step from, and into glass.

Short Stories

"Lover, you are the child I will never
Have . . . *have* had . . . *will* have," she wrote.
That was in Denver. October or November.
Long before she married a lawyer.
They're living, now, unhappily forever.

   He was writing in Greece, and from:
   " 'In the time it took not to get to the castle,
   Space developed its chronic asthma . . .'
   I'm fleeing with the cat to Hydra.
   Escapes and such have gorgeous results.
   I'm giving it up. Can't write at all.
   So long. And scratch one nightingale."

If you climb to the top of a bank building
In Denver, the highest one around,
All you can see for miles are mountains.
Banks and insurance companies have
The money to build and build and build.
"The *hell* with architecture," he said—
A trustee of The Wheat and Bread
Amalgamated Holding Co.—
"Get a contractor. And let's go."
His wife was home, drinking again.
She thought: I mustn't forget to eat.

   "It is the dumb, intractable
   Retarded who are sexual
   And hold the mystery in their hands . . ."
   A professor wrote, after his class.
   Revised, rewritten, then recast
   Into the form of a Gothic novel
   About a nun who meets the devil,
   Bewitches him—the usual *kitsch*—
   Half put-on and half spiritual,

It sold over a million copies
And made the professor very rich.

Meanwhile, a thousand miles away,
On a bulletin board at IBM's
Six hundred thousandth factory,
The following message found its way:
"If anyone hears of a small, unfurnished
Air-conditioned person . . ."

"Children, you are the lovers I
Could never get," she almost said
Under her breath, which was just as well
Since it was nine-tenths alcohol.
"It's time for another drink, I guess.
Yes? . . . No. . . . No? . . . Yes."

In Greece, he started to write again,
"The Underground Sonnets" in four-beat lines:
"And I would find it hard to say
Who went where and who which way,"
Interrupted by the arrival of
One of the Greek hoodlums of love . . .

The following month his editor wrote,
"*An*drew, *what* is *hap*pening to you?
You know the ms. is unpublishable . . ."

The professor, after his first success,
Went back to poetry. Which did not, alas,
Return the compliment. And so he wrote
A book of comic meditations
Filched from sources not hard to trace.
He was saved by tenure and an understanding
Dean, spent six weeks at a *place*,

Where everyone was nice but the nurses.
The doctor said, "It's no disgrace . . ."

In Denver, the hotel bar's discreet.
A layman (ha ha) would never know
What's going on, it looks so straight.
After it closes . . . *you* know . . .
A little car on a back street,
And so forth.

"People aren't really built to stand
The kind of tension you get these days;
Betrayal in personal relationships
Is the very worst, of course, because
The Oedipal syndrome is revived again . . .
I think that guilt, not fear's the thing
For which we pay the highest cost;
I, personally, find it hard to feel
Guilty—except at not feeling guilt . . ."

The professor listened but wasn't cured
And produced that long, astonishing book,
Counting Sheep or The Shepherd's Crook:
Deviation on the Western Plains,
Which has just come out as a paperback
With an introduction by a poet back
From Greece . . .

She read it in a nursing home,
Having arrived at the same place
The professor recently left. And soon
They dried her out and sent her home.
She's fine in public now "but not
So hot in bed," the trustee said—
The trustee of the Wheat and Bread.

"One more poem, one more try,"
The prof to the poet said, whose sly
Rejoinder was, "With me, it's vi-
ce versa . . ."

One night, back on the sauce, she said,
Looking the trustee straight in the eye,
"*You* are the death I would never have,
I *thought* . . ."

The message on the bulletin board
Has had several replies, but none
Satisfactory. And yesterday
It disappeared. Or was thrown away.

IV

The Skaters' Waltz

I'd like to hear The Skaters' Waltz again
And see Vienna on my TV set
With pictures of the King and Queen I love.
What is it makes them all so dear to me?
The skaters' icy skill, the dancers' verve?
I do not know if that's a polished floor
Or a pond so brightly lit that, in its glare,
Inverted on the brilliant ice, the world
Is hanging like a crystal chandelier
Ready to be dropped or be drawn up
In one quick graceful gesture. But I fear
When it goes up or down that so will we.
That's why on winter nights, and summer, too,
The thing above all else I like to do
Is listen to The Skaters' Waltz again,
Because as long as all the dancers turn,
I think they'll play it on and on and on . . .

Cats and Dogs: A Study in Race Relations

In Pusseyville, where pussies live,
The hangdog dogs on the dog days
Would disappear. They'd fade into the hills,
Lounge on the garbage heaps, slouch on quais,

Down in the dumps at the docks. A cat,
Real cool, I knew, would sip iced tea
Laced with a bit of barbiturate,
An illustrated dog book on her knee,

And say, "For no amount of scratch
Will dogs by day broach my backyard.
Pusseyville for pussies!" That old wretch!
When night had turned its black ace card,

What matings as the fur flew, yowl and bark,
Above the radio's blurred monologues.
And visitors would say, who risked the dark,
"In Pusseyville, it's raining cats and dogs!"

Celery

Sampans
So wet
They are
The stuff
They drown in,

How could
They know
They are
Dying
For salt?

Geraniums

(Based on an article in the 11th edition of the
Encyclopedia Britannica)

These herbs of annual or perennial duration
Dispersed throughout the world in the temperate zone
Are all of a nature highly ornamental.
Their favorite soil is a fibrous loam
With rotted stable manure or leaf-mold
Not to be sifted but pulled to pieces by hand,
And, so moisture may pass through it freely, sand.

Fine specimens grow best from half-ripened shoots
More delicate in structure than the zonal varieties;
Impatient of excess water at the root,
These, for bedding purposes, are usually struck
Toward the middle of August in the open air
And evolved from some of the species from the Cape
They include French spotted flowers and the market type.

On the Difficulty of Obtaining
Potions

There are enchanting remedies, they say,
That heroines and heroes of the past
Would take to make themselves feel mad or gay,
And though the drugs' effects would seldom last,
Their pulses, pharmaceutically fast,
Could spin day into night, night into day,
Or slow time down to one long matinée.

Tristan, entranced by what was in his cup,
Unclear, but sensual, drank to the dregs.
Isolde, passionate, forgot her nup-
tials, and lost King Mark and her sea legs.
A pharmacist I know always reneges
When asked for a love potion. "It's corrup-
t," he says. "Try alcohol. Bottoms up!"

As split as any split infinitive,
Dr. Jekyll—Mr. Hyde, *au fond*—
Soon found his heady drink imperative;
A great physician, in the demi-monde
Transfixed, gorilla-ish, he chased a blonde.
My druggist says, "That is no way to live.
You wouldn't like it. Try a sedative."

I now despair of ever getting some
Of either potion. And why drink it down?
Though nice to have a beau ideal succumb,
And never have to go out on the town,
Equinal is fast, and so's Miltown,
And being much too calm now, much too numb,
And potionless, *dormito ergo sum*.

Lunch at the Beach

*"I don't care what I eat, as long as it's the same
every day."* WITTGENSTEIN

Luncheon was always tuna salad
Served at the beach with an almost gelid
Cold consommé too soon unjellied
For, by the time, of course, we belted it
Down, the summer sun had melted it.
Mother'd make it, pack it, and take it
Down to the beach in a wicker basket,
Open it, pass it around, and ask if
The tuna was better than *yes*terday's tuna—
It seemed quite important. My sister, Shirley,
Asked why our diet couldn't be varied.
Mother would say but it *was*, to taste the
Difference between tuna chunks and paste, the
Difference—so obvious to *her*—was startling.
Tomorrow, there'd be a surprise; she was starting—
In her own mind—not a *pallid* salad
Made with celery, but with a shallot
Slivered fine she'd pound with a mallet.

At dusk, on the porch, I'd whisper, "Shirley . . ."
Mother'd appear with a bowl, say, "Try it!",
Then disappear. Then I'd say, "Shirley,
It's not *my* idea of a varied diet."
Shirley would say, "It's so uninspiring—
Tuna and soup. Was Wittgenstein lying?
Let's get her a grant, get her commissioned
To make something new. Roast beef? Custard?"
And then, one day, inside the basket,
Mother packed sandwiches of cold brisket
Thinly sliced—on rye—with mustard.
Naturally Shirley and I wouldn't risk it,
Being, like Pavlov's dog, conditioned.

So *Shirley* said, "I think I'd sooner
Die than eat brisket. Where's the tuna?"
And, after that, not to put too fine a
Point on the story, starting in June, a
Lunch at the beach was always tuna.

A Problem in Morals

Promiscuous lovers
Pine to have,
Under the covers,
One faithful love,
And treat their lust,
Being overwrought,
With rare disgust
On second thought.

Faithful lovers
Soon develop
The eye of rovers—
Satyr, trollop,
Long out of mind,
Become enticing
And come around:
The cake needs icing.

Though most have tried
A bit of both,
Lied and denied,
And nothing loth
To lie again,
They've never found,
With women and men,
A middle ground.

Romantic Love: A Footnote

The ill-used sea
And its ancient laundry
Tosses up a dirty
Wash or two,
Which puts in question
Thoughts of eternity:
Grapefruit and tar
Are not incredible blue.

Somebody ought to raise
A banner for
A possible life,
A dirty sea floor,
The general seediness
Of all good things
That do not glide like swans
Or sit like kings.

Bores

(To a child who asked what a "bore" was)

A bore is someone very boring.
The matter needs no underscoring.
For instance, if you're on a train,
You'll madly look around in vain
For someone interesting to chat with
And soon regret the one you sat with,
And if you summer on the shore, you
Soon will find someone to bore you,
And even on a mountain top,
Some lady, talking without a stop,
Will tell you just how *fright*fully you
Bore her when what's *really* true
Is the reverse: *She* bores *you.*
And what is true, essentially,
Is everyone potentially
Is boring, as you'll find when you're
Grown up and you're your*self* a bore.

The End of Words:
An Election-Year Thought

Drive past in the night; the two white lions
Of the library crouch, quite unaware
Of deficit financing, of literary lions
Working the moonlit salons of uptown
Going downhill fast. And so it's time
To fall in love with the first lip reader
You meet, avoiding the ever-present falseness
Of language. What will there be left to read?
Nothing. Yet it's better than pretending
Those deadly cackles are some form of speech,
To go on speaking, endlessly defending
Feelings never felt, words now dead,
Distorted, or misused. Other suggestions:
Writing poems in math, pressing flowers
Between blank pages of a book, or finding
Manuscripts among our future ruins
Untranslated from the original Garbage,
That tongue that power captured for the world
Which is now the only utterance of statesmen.

Charm

Intelligence endures
The sea-shake of the heart,
Its flops and opening nights,
But the body's theater alone
Eludes even its playwrights:
Too soon the script is done,
The curtain down. Applause.
Bravo! Encore! The lights . . .
And a rush to the doors.

Because the world's police
Have instinct on the books,
Innocence is nice
But not for long. Good looks
Turn bad, and time's as famous
For playing dirty tricks
As virtue is, whose price
Is beautifully to skate
On increasingly thin ice.

The beauties of the brain
And body are not charm—
Though charming they can be.
Charm is a sympathy
That sometimes draws a line
Under the unProfound
By an irony of tone,
And it is mostly missed
Once it is heard and gone.

Old bones know charm the best;
They see the trees for the wood,
The shades at their light task,
The magical latitude
That time cannot redress;

Their knowledge is their loss:
Under the worldly mask
They take off at their risk
They feel the pull of childhood.

Life adds up to not much.
Subtracted every day
Another sparrow falls
Oblivious from its perch.
That truth lacks charm, it's true,
Directly looked at, but
There is that version which
Can sometimes sound the depths
With the lightest touch.

V

The Refrigerator

The argument of the refrigerator wakes me.
It is trying to tell me it doesn't want to be cold,
It never wanted to be cold, it didn't choose
This life where everyone around it hates it.
"People only use me for their own convenience,"
It says. With a shudder, it starts off again,
Undergoing an electrical seizure,
Rambling on about its hurts and troubles:
People think it's heartless, stolid, frigid,
When, deep down, it craves for warmth and wants . . .
Well, it hesitates to say it, but
All it *really* wants is to be a stove.
Oh, how it dreams each night of the paired
Gas jets switching on their tropical blue,
The swoosh just after the match catches on,
The rectangular, passionate grid of flame
In the oven, the romance of changing things
Into other things. "The egg of the Real
Becoming the soufflé of the Ideal—
That's what I call the creative life."

"You perform an important function," I say,
"Without you, where would we be, these days . . ."
"Yes, yes, I know," it impatiently replies,
"But do you"—pause—"think I'm attractive?"
My silence, I fear, gives the show away.
"Of course," I stumble on, "for what you do,
You're remarkably well made, so few things work . . ."
Coldly, it opens, then slams its door.
"I didn't mean . . ." I say. But it will not respond.
At midnight, with a premeditated click,
It detaches itself from the circuits of the world,
Manages to shut itself off completely,
And gives up the ghost. By morning, all is lost.
"Damn it," I say to my coffee, black

(The milk's turned sour overnight),
"Unfullfillment's claimed yet another victim,"
Just as the stove speaks up to say,
"Do you think? . . . I hear . . . in the frozen north . . ."

Companies

God bless Con Ed, I've always said
As the gas flames bubbled up,
I brew my tea and toast my bread,
Whether I breakfast, lunch, or sup,
On power that Con Ed supplies,
And under the macadam's crust,
When cables break and wire dies,
It always digs because it must.

God bless the New York Tele. Co.
That keeps *its* wires free,
And has nice girls who say hello
(And say it so distinctly),
And sends one letters, half in tears,
Saying it only meant to be—
In regard to a payment in arrears—
A little struggling monopoly.

But God bless IBM the most,
For it computes the final cost
Of telephones and tea and toast
And has on checks one's code embossed
In heiroglyphs that can't be read
Because the zeroes all are straight,
Yet manages to say, instead,
"Don't fold, spindle, or mutilate."

Circle

Now are we saying goodbye?
I think so but can't be sure.
The last phone call but one
Left everything up in the air.
When you called last, did you mean
What you said when you said you meant
To say that this call would be
The last if I didn't call?
In fact, I'm not sure at all
If you called or I called you back.
And did you say "goodbye,"
Or I say "good night" and you
Say "Do you mean 'good night'
Or 'goodbye'?" I think it was you.
And what were you trying to do
When you said, "*You* said we're through?"
How could that be since you
Were the first to bring it up?
I don't think it's what *I* said,
Though you keep saying I did.
In any case, now that you know
That you know what I meant to say,
Why don't you say what you mean?
I mean if you mean to say
That the last call was the last.
I think that that would be best.
If something is finished, it's just
As well to get up and go.
If you're interested still to know,
I like a slate wiped clean,
And if you would pick up the phone,
I'd tell you what I mean.

Boiling Eggs

My waking hunger wants its hourglass
Turned upside down to clock my boiling eggs.
   Bobbing about, they've lost their sea legs,
   And though no theorem of Pythagoras,
      Prove, by that stately 8,
That even early birds can be too late,
For appetite requires that these yet unborn
Chicks give up the ghost this wintry morn.

One more minute now. How I regret (poor chicks!)
To take them out of Nature so that I may dine.
   Theirs is a fate that my arithmetic's
   Not wholly to be blamed for—the Great Design,
      Mother Nature, not my clock,
Prescribes for hens the ardor of the cock—
Some learn, from experience, how one good egg
Can scramble up a lifetime. Were I to renege,

Ponder still their ends: cock or hen,
(Or worse, a capon), at the finish line
   Meets a grisly doom. Who's to say when
   They'd vanish dimly down the throats of men?
      The end cannot be breached:
For whether eggs are coddled, baked, or poached,
Or Benedict or fried or served Foo Yung,
They make a tasty morsel for the tongue.

They're done. I put them in a tablespoon,
One by one, beneath the water tap
   To cool, and when I break the lime cocoon,
   The membrane curls away, a tattered map.
      Mingled in a cup,
Buttered, salted, peppered, I scoop them up,
Who are not what they were. Now they're uncased,
I cannot tell a lie: I like the taste.

The hourglass, standing on my pantry shelf,
Immune to both my hunger and their state,
   Diurnally is fated to reverse itself
   And time two boiling eggs at the same rate.
      Satiety can't last:
The ultimate in feasts leads to a new repast—
Tomorrow when my hourglass is turned about,
Appetite will dine again, and time run out.

A Limited View or
Small Domestic Essay

It is your weakness more than your strength
That ultimately tells you who you are—
Whatever you love will kill or save you.
You give up the sublime, walk into the kitchen,
And meet it there—its domestic version,
A short order cook of the precious inane.

Yes precious, for being absurd or vulgar
Or funny or risky or even audacious,
The wry movie made from the tedious thriller,
The sad anecdote whose one witty angle
Changes a tearful roomful of people
Into one which is having a mildly good time.

I am talking about waking up in the morning
Not feeling depressed, of reaching over
To feel affection under passion's cover
With one who laughs a lot and is not a glum one
With silences denoting disapproval
Or oddball rages that arrive from nowhere,

The end of judging, not the end of judgment,
Lunches for which one doesn't pay in small talk,
Dinner companions reasonably amusing,
Clothes that fit and are also attractive,
And a house, not necessarily the best in town,
In which, in the evening, your dog is happy.

The Private Elevator

We were trying to get from the third to the second
Floor in a private elevator and
Were amazed to find ourselves suddenly trapped—
All twenty-two of us. The town house belonged
To two psychiatrists away on vacation,
And whether we had had, or were about to have dinner
Never became clear. Since the elevator held
Four at the most, Causely and Marian
Tried to get out to make room for the others,
But misunderstood—as so many times before—
They caused a slight disturbance on the stair
Where hundreds were standing waiting in a queue.
Only I, I think, had the wit to look for
What couldn't, in the end, be found—a phone.
And ALARM was disconnected. So I said,
Trying to be cheerful, "Full speed ahead!"
The light was watery but slightly dirty
Like the cabbage soup served to prisoners of war.
Terence wore a cornflower in his buttonhole.
Marcia swore when she tore her Balenciaga.
Everyone seemed to want to get in bed
With someone bigger, like a mother or a father.
Cynthia made the disquieting discovery
That the stairs leading up led absolutely nowhere,
And Osbert that the stairs leading *down* led nowhere.
We were in some sort of stageset suspended in mid-air,
And what had looked like Fifth Avenue and solid trees
Turned out to be cloud formations in the sky
Already aroused by malignant thunder.
Symptoms became evident—breathing difficulties,
Hardships of balance, and stomach spasms.
Lula got panicky and screamed. Stuart said
He kept thinking of tunnels, subways, and other
Underground traps. Edward coughed wildly.
Cold bothered William and Jennifer, heat

Daniel and Mirabelle. "How the hell
Are we going to get out of here?" Beatrice asked,
Exhibiting an unsuspected flair for coolness.
Elvira, who had nerves of aluminum, laughed.
I looked for some oil, locks, keys, a crowbar,
But Gloria found some damp carbon paper
On which we all wrote our names . . . in case . . .
Stronger than the fear of death was the fear
Of embarrassment, the loss of bodily functions.
Rosalind was the first to commit a nuisance.
"The social codes are breaking down," Otis said
Stupidly. Peggy demanded to be rescued.
Philip and Sydney and, of course, myself
Were the ones who found the elevator potion,
Releasing us all at exactly 8 A.M.
To a ringing of bells and an official welcome.
The evening was, retrospectively, festive,
Which is why it seemed rather sinister when,
Ten years later, in *The New York Times*'s
Obituary column, twenty-one of us were listed
Under identical headlines: Buried Alive.

A Ship Going Down

It wasn't in the script.
Descending like fast kites,
A frigate's sails collapsed;
A spluttering of lights

From the bulb behind the film
Shipwrecked the shipwreck,
Burned the burning helm,
And engulfed the whole deck.

When all the lights went out,
The sea, rushing up the screen,
Blacked out. A total night,
Erasing the mezzanine,

Swept up to the balcony
And darkened the vacant seats.
We walked out into the lobby
For candy and cigarettes.

(The film had become uncoiled.
The projectionist, meanwhile,
Frantically reeled and reeled
It back onto the spool.)

"I think when we go back in
We'll have a change of luck—
The proud ship sails on . . .
Somehow they undo the wreck . . .

In spite of reality,
For that four-rigger, Hope,
Can sail the seven seas
Until all hands give up."

A Thank-You Note for Imaginary Gifts

*Thank you, Juliette Marglen, for your gift of lovelier
lips and fingertips.*
                    Advertisement in *The New Yorker*

Thank you, Juliette Marglen,
For your gift of lovelier lips
    And fingertips—
    And whisky sips,
    And cocktail dips,
    Also calyps-
    o songs, and, *ips-*
    o facto, tips
    On horses, grips
    We pack for trips,
    The old Poughkeeps-
    ie station, rips
    In nylons, whips
    In Senates, gyps-
    y camps, ellips-
    es, paper clips,
    The Apocalypse,
    And garden thrips.
Who *are* you, Juliette Marglen?

Who *are* you, Juliette Marglen,
With your gift of lovelier lips
     And fingertips
     And chops and chips
     And slips and slops
     And bops and quips
     And skips and hops
     And shops and ships
     And hips and crops
     And fops and drips
     And pips and pops
     And sops and scrips
     And flips and flops
     And tops and strips
     And gyps and cops
     And mops and props
     And drops and snips
     And nips of schnapps?
Thank *you*, Juliette Marglen.

Horror Movie

Dr. Unlikely, we love you so,
You who made the double-headed rabbits grow
From a single hare. Mutation's friend,
Who could have prophecied the end
When the Spider Woman deftly snared the fly
And the monsters strangled in a monstrous kiss
And somebody hissed, "You'll hang for this!"?

Dear Dracula, sleeping on your native soil
(Any other kind makes him spoil),
How we clapped when you broke the French door down
And surprised the bride in the overwrought bed.
Perfectly dressed for lunar research,
Your evening cape added much,
Though the bride, inexplicably dressed in furs,
Was a study in jaded jugulars.

Poor, tortured Leopard Man, you changed your spots
In the debauched village of the Pin-Head Tots;
How we wrung our hands, how we wept
When the eighteenth murder proved inept,
And, caught in the Phosphorous Cave of Sea,
Dangling the last of synthetic flesh,
You said, "There's something wrong with me."

The Wolf Man knew when he prowled at dawn
Beginnings spin a web where endings spawn.
The bat who lived on shaving cream,
A household pet of Dr. Dream,
Unfortunately maddened by the bedlam,
Turned on the Doc, bit the hand that fed him.

And you, Dr. X, who killed by moonlight,
We loved your scream in the laboratory
When the panel slid and the night was starry
And you threw the inventor in the crocodile pit
(An obscure point: Did he deserve it?)
And you took the gold to Transylvania
Where no one guessed how insane you were.

We thank you for the moral and the mood,
Dear Dr. Cliché, Nurse Platitude.
When we meet again by the Overturned Grave
Near the Sunken City of the Twisted Mind
(In *The Son of the Son of Frankenstein*),
Make the blood flow, make the motive muddy:
There's a little death in every body.

Howard Moss

Howard Moss is the poetry editor of *The New Yorker*.
Before joining its staff in 1948, he was an instructor
of English at Vassar College. The author of eight
earlier books of poems, and two books of criticism,
The Magic Lantern of Marcel Proust and *Writing Against
Time,* he has also edited the poems of Keats, the
nonsense verse of Edward Lear, and a collection of
short stories written by poets, *The Poet's Story.*
A play, *The Folding Green,* was first produced by
The Poets' Theater in Cambridge, Mass., and then
by the Playwrights' Unit in New York City, and a
more recent work, *The Palace at 4 A.M.,* was produced
in the summer of 1972 at the John Drew Theater
in East Hampton, with Edward Albee as its director.
In the same year, Moss received the National Book
Award for his *Selected Poems.* In 1974, he published a
book of satirical biographies, *Instant Lives* with
drawings by Edward Gorey. Moss is a member of
The National Institute of Arts and Letters and
received a grant in creative writing from that
organization in 1968.